ISSUES IN GOVERNANCE FOR
PERFORMANCE-BASED TEACHER EDUCATION

by Michael W. Kirst
Stanford University
Stanford, California

for the AACTE

Committee on Performance-Based Teacher Education

October 1973

American Association of Colleges for Teacher Education
One Dupont Circle
Washington, D. C. 20036

This paper was prepared pursuant to a contract with the
United States Office of Education, through the Texas
Education Agency, Austin, Texas. The opinions expressed
herein should not be construed as representing the opinions
of the United States Government or the Texas Education
Agency.

Library of Congress Catalog Card Number: 73-87764

Standard Book Number: 910052-77-8

Preface

The American Association of Colleges for Teacher
Education is pleased to publish this paper as one of a
series sponsored by its Committee on Performance-Based
Teacher Education. The series is designed to expand the
knowledge base about issues, problems, and prospects
regarding performance-based teacher education as identified
in the first publication of the series on the state of the
art.[1]

Whereas the latter is a declaration for which the
Committee accepts full responsibility, publication of this
paper (and the others in the PBTE Series) does not imply
Association or Committee endorsement of the views expressed.
It is believed, however, that the experience and expertise
of these individual authors, as reflected in their writings,
are such that their ideas are fruitful additions to the con-
tinuing dialogue concerning performance-based teacher education.

One of the challenging problem areas associated with the
implementation of PBTE programs is overcoming the governance
and political issues which surround its implementation. The
PBTE Committee noted in its first paper that "the PBTE movement could deteriorate into a power struggle over who controls
what. Thus there is a need to specify decision-making roles
early, to work out political and legal relationships satis-
factorily, or to evolve new organizations and institutions
where the cleavages will not exist..." The Committee commis-
sioned the author to examine these and other questions, and
this publication represents his analysis and interpretation.
We believe that this study, which focuses on such major issues
as accreditation, broadening the decision-making base, and the
role of the liberal arts, makes a significant contribution to
the PBTE series.

AACTE acknowledges with appreciation the role of the
National Center for Improvement of Educational Systems
(NCIES) of the U. S. Office of Education in the PBTE Project.
Its financial support as well as its professional stimulation
are major contributions to the Committee's work. The
Association acknowledges also the contribution of members of

---

[1]Elam, Stanley, Performance-Based Teacher Education: What
Is the State of the Art? The American Association of Colleges
for Teacher Education, December 1971.

the Committee who served as readers of this paper and of members of the Project staff who assisted in its publication. Special recognition is due J. W. Maucker, chairman of the Committee, David R. Krathwohl, member of the Committee, and Shirley Bonneville, member of the Staff, for their contributions to the development of the PBTE Series of monographs.

Edward C. Pomeroy,
Executive Director, AACTE

Karl Massanari,
Associate Director, AACTE,
Director, AACTE's Performance-Based
Teacher Education Project

Introductory Note

Any new movement upsets the status quo. The change may cause certain groups to become active in areas where they previously only voiced interest. The upset balance of power provides an opportunity for those who have been critical of established positions to make their views known, to assert their values and to bid for a part of the action. The performance-based teacher education (PBTE) movement is no exception. Thus, teachers who have long voiced an interest in teacher education and felt some responsibility for being active in it, find they can no longer afford so passive a posture. Although the major development of PBTE has been almost entirely at the undergraduate preservice level, performance criteria appropriate for graduates of such programs clearly have relevance for re-certification, for tenure decisions, and for other personnel actions of in-service teachers. Teachers therefore feel that they have a stake in the development of performance criteria and their measures.

Similarly, teacher aides, who believe that qualified members of the teaching profession should be without the long road through college to certification, have a stake in PBTE. They seek the establishment of performance criteria which they might be able to fulfill without that lengthy and expensive period of training. They would be very unhappy if criteria were set so that they were automatically excluded again. From just these two examples, it is apparent that the implications of PBTE vary from group to group, and that many groups have a stake in its development. The governance, that is the means by which the movement is nurtured, blunted, or otherwise controlled, is, therefore, an issue of considerable consequence.

From the outset, one important goal of these invited papers has been to tease out the implications of PBTE so that interested persons may consider its possibilities and problems, with some foreknowledge of consequences. Two early papers in the series, those by Andrews, and Cooper and Weber,* projected scenarios of what PBTE might in time become. Although the Andrews paper notes important roles for state and school, a full analysis of governance structure could not be fully developed in these papers. Accordingly, it was decided to find someone with competence in both education and political science to analyze the situation. We found this in Michael Kirst.

His analysis of the past role of accreditation and who controlled it sets the scene for what is happening today. His description of current activities bring many of us up to date on

the struggles and discussions that have been taking place. Finally,
his projections for the future suggest some possibilities for
conflict resolution, as well as some of the complexities with which
these possibilities confront us.

                    David R. Krathwohl, Member of the
                    PBTE Committee and chairman of its
                    Task Force on Commissioning Papers

---

*"Manchester Interview: Competency-Based Teacher Education/
Certification" by Theodore Andrews and "Competency-Based
Teacher Education: A Scenario" by James Cooper and Wilford Weber

Contents

ISSUES IN GOVERNANCE FOR
PERFORMANCE-BASED TEACHER EDUCATION

Overview

This paper will outline some of the major features of the
present policy-making system for teacher training, certification, and promotion as a basis for assessing changes that
the performance-based system might and should bring. As the
second section points out, some of these changes are inherent
in the concept of PBTE. Since the performance concept is
still being refined and undergoing considerable experimentation,
however, the analysis must be of a somewhat prescriptive and
speculative nature.

The author proceeds from a political approach, e.g., the
values and interests of the major parties involved will conflict and the outcome will entail bargaining, coalitions and
compromises. Moreover, value conflicts will often be embedded
in what heretofore have been regarded as professional/
technical decisions. Consequently, it will be exceedingly
difficult (perhaps impossible) to separate lay decisions from
professional decisions; or administration from policy. The
performance concept does not imply incremental change, so
consequently the value conflicts will be widespread. PBTE
would necessitate changes in every part of the present policy-
making system - e.g. preservice certification, career advance-
ment and development, employment criteria, recertification,
college curriculum, etc. - during a very contentious period
of our history. The outcome of this political activity
surrounding PBTE will probably be a realignment of the present
governance system of shared powers, but influence will still
reside in several groups and interests.

This paper outlines initially the evolution of the
governing structure for teacher education and certification.
This provides the context for analyzing the impact and probable
issues caused by PBTE.

The Evolution of the Present Governance System:
Certification and Accreditation

No political scientist has undertaken a historical
investigation of the present governance and influence structure for teacher education and certification.[1] The researcher

must piece it together from several secondary sources. For instance, Donald Cottrell has provided a useful bibliography of accreditation. His sources stress the gradual evolution of the locus of control, from countries to states and finally to professors through NCATE (The National Council for Accreditation of Teacher Education).[2]

Some observers point out the diversity of certification policies and governance systems among the states. But these state systems differ more in detail than in general approach or basic standards. Professional educators through several mechanisms stressed below succeeded in considerable standardization of certification and accreditation by 1960. In effect, a centralized influence structure of private organizations assumed the dominant role. Within any state, however, the formal prerogatives are held by the state department of education (SDE's) acting under general rules promulgated by the state board and/or legislature. Often there is more latitude in the present system than the rules imply because SDE's can interpret the same general standards in different ways.[3]

The influence linkage between certification and university teacher training content is direct and pervasive. The detailed certification requirements in California, for example, are reflected in specific university course titles and help determine the overall program orientation.

First, the states with their active interest in certification want to know the minimum number of quarter or semester hours of work required for majors and minors in teacher education programs..Second, the states are interested in the general education or general degree requirements of teacher education institutions. Here the states are concerned not only with the total requirement, but also with the general area or division of subject matter, such as English, mathematics..Like the regional associations, the states as a rule do not concern themselves with teaching methods employed in presenting the subject matter, whether in survey courses, lecture courses, seminars, or discussion groups...

If the state issues certificates by 'credit counting' and the state requires four hours in mathematics, the teacher education institutions of the state feel obliged to offer a

four-credit-hour course in mathematics, even
though a three- or five-hour course might be
preferred by the department of mathematics.[4]

If the states and the institutions of higher education
were only actors in the policy-making system our task would be
easier, and this interstate diversity would be more fundamental.
Once the university educators become organized, however, they
assumed the primary role in determining accreditation standards
for higher education and thereby determined the orientation
and general approach of state certification requirements.[5]
Organizations of classroom teachers were slow to assert their
influence in this area and challenge the evolving state and
university hegemony. But in the 70's new forces are on the
move such as classroom teachers and, as we shall see, they will
have great impact on PBTE.

The Growth of NCATE: Hegemony by Professors

In his history of teacher education, Stinnett justifies
NCATE as a response to several problems confronting teachers.

> State accrediting was found to be too diverse.
> In many instances state accrediting agencies
> were unable, because of political and other
> pressures, to impose discriminating standards
> upon colleges and universities wishing to en-
> gage in teacher education. Thus, the quality
> of teacher education programs ranged from
> superb to the ludicrous. Reciprocity in
> teacher certification among the states, be-
> cause of the diversity of requirements, led
> to regional reciprocity compacts, but these
> were relatively ineffective; and teachers,
> highly qualified and broadly experienced,
> as they transferred to another state, ran
> into heavy assessments of deficiencies to be
> made up by further college work.[6]

Out of this context emerged NEA's National Commission on
Teacher Education and Professional Standards. Out of joint
planning of AACTE, TEPS, the Council of Chief State School
Officers, and the National School Boards Association emerged
NCATE. Teachers who graduated from NCATE-accredited institu-
tions were given reciprocity of certification as they crossed
state lines. Obviously, the "professional standards" that
NCATE used to accredit institutions had a tremendous impact on

3

the direction and content of teacher education. By 1970, NCATE-accredited institutions numbered 470, preparing four-fifths of the new teachers. NCATE's pervasive influence led to several counterattacks such as James Koerner's criticism:

> But, most of all, NCATE was criticized for its power politics. It was censured for pressuring institutions into applying for accreditation, for encouraging professional associations of various kinds to restrict their membership to graduates of NCATE-accredited programs, for persuading their fellow professional educators in state departments of education to discriminate against teachers who applied for a license from non NCATE schools...[7]

For our purposes here, who controlled NCATE is especially important. Stinnett shows how the restructuring of the NCATE's Council concentrated influence in institutions of higher education.

TABLE I

Representation, NCATE	1954	1956	1966
1. Practitioners	6	6	6
2. Colleges and Universities	6	7	10
3. State Legal Authorities	6	2	2
4. Local Legal Authorities	3	1	1
5. Academic Disciplines	0	3	3
Total	21	19	22

Including the representation of the academic disciplines, institutions of higher education expanded their representation from 6 to 13 while the 2 million public school practitioners remain at six and the legal education authorities were reduced from nine to three. If PBTE were governed by this kind of structure, its form and substance would probably be quite different than if the above representational proportions were reversed.

4

A System of Shared Powers

In the late 1950's the federal government and private foundations entered this arena of teacher education to add their influence to the established actors - state government, professional associations, and NCATE. Federal and foundation interest focused on innovations in a categorical way. Ford Foundation supported massively the MAT (Master of Art in Teaching) concept. The Federal role began with stimulating changes in curriculum content for teachers in math and sciences under NDEA and encouraging a larger role for the academic disciplines in teacher education. Recently, the Federal Education Professions Development Act has stressed demonstration reform programs such as the Teacher Corps, Triple T, and Career Opportunities (new career ladders). Federal policy has also encouraged parental and student influence in teacher training through such devices as Title I-ESEA and Model Cities. In 1970, for example, USOE mounted a program in Urban/Rural School Development that features a parity board of parents and teachers to determine policy and content for in-service training. Recently EPDA funds have gone directly to local schools, by-passing the traditional route of teacher training institutions.

This increase in federal influence through experimental teacher training programs highlighted the lessening influence of NCATE. Several challenges to NCATE's standards began in the early sixties by some prestige universities and groups of liberal arts professors. In particular, the University of Wisconsin under Dean Lindley Stiles declared his institution would not seek NCATE's approval until the criteria were changed. Liberal arts professors claimed NCATE's standards neglected the strength of the universities' overall resources and concentrated on quantity of education faculty, education libraries, etc. This type of pressure led to more flexible and broader NCATE standards plus the reconstitution of NCATE's policy board. Liberal arts professors gained representation and, as Table I demonstrated, this further lessened the influence of classroom teachers and state and local education authorities. As we shall see, this jockeying for influence over the content of teacher education between liberal arts and education professors will continue with PBTE. NCATE approved several teacher training programs like the USOE experiments. The more flexible NCATE standards also promoted more diversity among state standards.

In 1972 a federally funded group of educators called the Committee on National Program Priorities in Teacher Education (CNPPTE) (headed by Professor Benjamin Rosner of CUNY) recommended a five year $150 million federal program to implement performance-based teacher education. As we shall see, several states encouraged the use of PBTE. Both NCATE and AACTE have encouraged experimentation and development of performance concepts. Indeed NCATE's standards (adopted 1970) include evaluation of graduate performance by institutions.

In sum, the present influence system, which performance-based teacher education will confront, is one of shared power among such organizations as: federal, state, and local governments, professional organizations, national accrediting associations (NCATE), foundations, and institutions of higher education (both academic disciplines and professional schools). Moreover, local schools conduct in-service programs and through their employment policies encourage certain types of preparation programs. Lay groups are represented somewhat through state legislatures and boards of education (state and local) and to a significant extent in some federal programs. Organized teacher groups traditionally have been influential at the state government level but unable to control NCATE. Students have not been a formal part of the apparatus except for their very recent and piecemeal impact on university governance bodies. But this constellation of power is in flux and PBTE will add to the realignments.

The historical evolution of this influence system has resulted in primacy for state government in formal certification. Individual universities have been designated by the states to prepare teachers and consequently have enjoyed considerable prerogatives. Professional influence through TEPS, AACTE, and NCATE developed primarily after the basic state legal structure was in place. The profession, at first through NCATE and subsequently through other methods of influence, has been able to set the fundamental criteria and general standards state governments use. Consequently, a foreign visitor would be more impressed by the similarities of teacher certification programs between, for example, Illinois and Mississippi than the detailed differences between these two states.

Governance Implications of PBTE

Introduction

PBTE is a different and controversial basis for teacher training and certification. If it could be implemented, it entails such fundamental changes that the present "balance of power" among the groups discussed above will be upset. All the actors and interests in the present system will see PBTE as an opening to enhance their control and institutionalize their particular value perspective. Given the present pluralistic distribution of influence, the emergence of a monopoly or dominant interest group is unlikely, but some groups will win in a relative sense and others lose. In part, the winners will be determined by national trends in educational politics that transcend the particular issues of PBTE. Such trends as militance and enhanced organization of classroom teachers and ethnic minorities will have important consequences. The national debate on tenure revision will spill over to PBTE.

What is this constellation of interests and value perspectives that will become involved in PBTE? A primary task for those who implement PBTE will be to decide on the precise objectives stated in behavioral terms and a specific catalog of priority skills and behaviors. Certainly, the advocates of informal education, open schools, and "humanism" will confront once again the "behaviorists" and "operant conditioners." In some ways the advocates of priority for the disciplines and "basic education" will tangle with a new breed of pedagogues. All shades of the conflicting philosophies of education will have a major stake in the outcome of PBTE. Given the base of research and state of the art, many of their differences can not be settled in the near future by empirical research findings. The outcome will probably entail considerable bargaining and compromise reflecting a number of philosophical viewpoints. The counterattack of the humanists in opposition to PBTE should not be underestimated.[8]

But joining the leaders of educational thought and researchers in the fray will be all the factions we see now struggling for control of U.S. educational policy - organized teachers, parents, ethnic minorities, students, legislators, and governors, foundation officials, federal bureaucrats, institutions of higher education, and other professional education groups (NEA , NCATE, AACTE, etc.). Most of these groups have a wide range of philosophical viewpoints within their memberships.

Impact on Researchers

A crucial unknown is whether the performance concept will lead to a new conceptual and validated research base for the elusive concept of "education profession." Some research strategies can be built into program design and implementation, but if PBTE is implemented before a large research base is in place, it will probably degenerate into an inchoate and elusive slogan that is used in negotiations among the contending forces. As one advocate of increased teacher influence put it:

> ...the really crucial question is whether teaching can be established on a validated knowledge base (as against conventional wisdom or experience validated) and whether the organized profession can become unified and strong enough to provide the teacher with authority to practice according to validated knowledge.[9]

Given this empirical uncertainty, the educational R & D community could play a larger role in PBTE than it did in NCATE or the formulation of current state policy. Very few researchers were influential in TEPS or NCATE, and heretofore state education agencies have not been known for their ability to translate research findings into public policy, but the researchers work slowly and their findings may take a decade or more. Meanwhile, we are confronted with widespread dissatisfaction with the present system of professional preparation and tenure with strong pressure for a short run "quick fix." Educators and government officials plunged into implementation of "accountability" and "accomplishment auditing" before the concept was clearly defined or based on validated knowledge.

Clearly, the educational R & D community has the opportunity to lead by collecting the data and establishing the criteria. An underlying premise of PBTE is that if teachers are trained to exhibit certain specific "competencies," they will be more effective in producing desired pupil attainments than teachers prepared in the traditional way. Obviously experimental designs will have to be undertaken to explore this premise, and to establish the preferred competencies. If PBTE is used for certification in the near future (as Texas and Washington propose), research will be used to modify standards, not establish them initially. Many researchers think the whole effort to establish teaching competencies is beyond the state of the art.[10]

Reaction of Teacher Organizations

Another group that will probably gain in relative influence with the advent of PBTE will be NEA and AFT organized classroom teachers. As we have seen, the NCATE - State Government alliance was composed more of university professors, higher education administrators, and long-term government employees. Classroom teachers, however, are better organized now than at the advent of NCATE and want to be spokesmen for themselves. As Howsam stresses:

> Accordingly, it follows that representation of the organized profession is critical. The difference between having teachers on committees, boards, and commissions with an employee orientation and without a professional mandate is subtle enough to have escaped attention in the past. It should not be perpetuated.[11]

Teacher leaders assert they are closest to classroom interaction and have a better grasp of classroom competencies than deans or professors. Moreover, if employment and promotion decisions are to be based on "performance," this will be a prime concern of teacher contract negotiations. Again we must acknowledge the possibility that technical difficulties of defining and demonstrating competence could be so important and value conflicts so irresolvable that PBTE will become merely a negotiating slogan between contending forces. Teacher organization leaders see PBTE as a method to break the hegemony of universities but are unsure of their precise negotiating demands in terms of substantive changes in PBTE concepts.

Some of the directions organized teachers want to pursue, however, are already emerging. They appear to favor even less influence for the disciplines as the comments below indicate:

> ...there should be considerably less emphasis on teacher education as an all-university function.
> (a) the teacher education subsystem is the one with primary responsibility for the professional preparation of teachers.
> (b) other university subsystems with a role in teacher education (the disciplines) are no more critical to teacher education than they are to the other professional schools. They provide instructional service to the professional schools.
> (c) effectively requiring education to jointly provide for the education of teachers with other units which have less interest and conflicting purposes makes education dependent and makes it responsible for behavior over which it has no control. [12]

PBTE implies more observation of teachers in the classroom, and it is unlikely that teacher organizations will have as little to say about this field component as they have in the past. Indeed teacher organizations want evaluation of classroom performance by peers of classroom teachers rather than by state or university "experts." This is likely to be their key demand, but its relationship to PBTE is as yet unclear.

At this point NEA is pushing for the organized classroom teachers to dominate teacher certification and training through a new state level professional standards unit independent of the state education agency. California's so-called Ryan Act has established such an independent commission appointed by the Governor with representatives from most of the contending interests mentioned previously. The 15-person commission has 6 certified teachers, 4 university faculty, 2 school board members, and 3 private citizens. Ex officio members are from the State Superintendent's Office, the Regents, and from other postsecondary boards. Each of these groups can make a legitimate claim for a place on a policy-making board and each has a somewhat different perspective on what PBTE should stress. Again, we come back to the unlikely event that research can settle the issues of which competencies should have priority, so any policy board will end up resolving these issues through bargaining, compromise, and probably some old fashioned log-rolling.

One teacher's view on current in-service training is expressed below.

> Practicing teachers have found it close to impossible to get the kind of continuing education which is relevant to their real problems. They have to pursue the advanced college degree route because such degrees have been tied to salary schedules by school board members who believe that completed college courses are the sole indicator of the quality of a teacher. Teachers must have the power to say what it is that they need to learn to keep up with changing times - and to be able, through state and local governance procedures, to see that they get it.[13]

If teachers are successful in separating "professional standards" from the State Department, it is important to probe the probable impact on PBTE. The professional's traditional viewpoint that educational policy should be separated from general government has been to increase the influence of professional educators vis-a-vis mayors, governors, city·councils, and state legislators. As we have seen, however, NCATE dominated by college educators had very close ties with SDE's. Consequently, the teacher groups must be hoping that they will be the professional group that will dominate the new professional standards boards. If this happens, PBTE could be vetoed by organized classroom teachers and can only succeed if key concessions are made to such groups. It would become more crucial for adherents of PBTE to have the enthusiastic backing of teacher organizations than the endorsement of key SDE officials, but this strategy will vary according to great differences in state politics. Teacher organizations in Florida are in disarray and not very strong, while New York is quite a different situation. It is likely, however, that teachers will have a greater role under new PBTE standards than in the past - both in setting the criteria and having teachers evaluate each other.

Politics within the University Teacher Trainers

The experiences with PBTE in Texas and Washington highlight the political threat of PBTE for liberal arts professors.[14] In Texas, where proposed legislation requires that all courses a prospective teacher takes, including those in the liberal arts, be performance-based, the liberal arts faculty has sponsored a counter-measure that would emasculate the state's thrust toward PBTE. This counter-measure would

1) make the universities solely responsible for teacher education rather than sharing power with teacher groups and local schools.

2) prohibit the state education department from requiring any approach (PBTE) for teacher training.

In effect, PBTE becomes a vehicle for shifting control from the campus to off-campus areas. In the past, cooperation with off-campus groups was permissive but now the Texas Competency-Based Teacher Education standards envision a tripartite council of campus, school system and organized profession. Many Texas liberal arts and subject matter professors claim this violates academic freedom. These liberal arts professors also cite AACTE publications showing PBTE has a "thin research base" and consequently should be delayed. School teacher and administrator groups organized under the banner of the Texas State Teachers' Association have supported the PBTE concept.

The Colleges of Education are, as one dean put it, "caught in the middle of the crossfire." They are seen by the liberal arts group as in collusion with the professional practitioners. But many teachers and administrators see College of Education

11

faculty as part of the campus trying to retain their historic
control. In Washington, PBTE has been underway since 1971.
One aspect of the reaction of the education faculty is indicated by this observation in a report on strengths and weaknesses of PBTE implementation.

> Competency-based teacher education is threatening
> to many college and school personnel. They do
> not feel they themselves are competent in the
> standards expected of candidates.[15]

The following resolution indicates the depth of feeling
among the liberal arts faculty in Texas.

RESOLUTION PASSED FOR ADOPTION BY THE
SOUTHWESTERN SOCIAL SCIENCE ASSOCIATION in Dallas, Texas
March 22-24, 1973

> WHEREAS, The Texas Education Agency has
> adopted, and several other central education
> agencies are moving in the direction of adopt-
> ing, administrative regulations that require all
> teacher education programs (including the
> academic disciplinary area) to conform to be-
> havioral or competency/performance-based objec-
> tives at both the undergraduate and graduate
> levels and that place ultimate control over
> selection of the objectives to be taught in
> the academic disciplinary areas in the hands
> of either the education school dean or an
> entity outside the university itself, be it

> RESOLVED, That the Southwestern Social
> Science Association expresses its alarm and
> opposition to any attempt by any individual,
> agency, or center outside the responsible
> academic faculty which seeks to control the
> form or content of instruction in academic
> social science courses in any discipline
> area either by the prescription of specific
> objectives or by the exercise of a veto power
> over whatever objectives may have been freely
> chosen by the concerned faculty members and,
> therefore, over the form and content of aca-
> demic instruction in social sciences courses
> and programs at the college and university
> levels; be it further

RESOLVED, That the Southwestern Social
Science Association rejects and deplores as
unwise, unwarranted, inimical to the most
rudimentary academic freedom of individual
professors, and destructive of the autonomy
and integrity of colleges and universities
in curricular matters the attempt by any
outside agency whatsoever to impose a
single, official teaching method or doctrine
upon students, teachers, and institutions
of higher education in a state and herewith
encourages its members in their personal
capacities to resist such imposition by
every means at their disposal; be it further

RESOLVED, That the Southwestern Social
Science Association earnestly petitions the
Texas State Board of Education to provide
alternatives to its imposition, upon the sixty
colleges and universities in that state engaged
in teacher education, of the controversial
and unproven ideology of competency/performance-
based teacher education and to withdraw, in
favor of a democratic and pluralistic approach
to teacher education, the "Teacher Certification Standards" promulgated in June, 1972,
premised on that doctrine; further, we com-
mend the recent decision of the Texas State
Board of Education to delay implementation
of these controversial new Standards until
1975 to permit restudy and revision of them;
and we urge that procedures promptly be established to provide for serious consultation
during this two-year period with accredited
representatives from the professional disciplines comprising this Association, with
similar recognized professional associations
in the other scientific and humane disciplines,
and with all segments of the academic community in Texas; and be it finally

RESOLVED, That the Southwestern Social
Science Association respecfully directs the
thoughtful attention of each of its members
and of all other concerned persons to the key
provisions of House Bill 1322 (now pending
before the Sixty-Third Texas Legislature)

which would immediately provide statutory
remedy if enacted: 'Each institution shall
be solely responsible for developing education programs to meet the requirements for
each authorized teaching certificate. The
(State) Board (of Education) may not require
an institution to teach a particular doctrine or to conduct instruction on the
basis of, or in accordance with, any particular pedagogical method, whether expressed in terms of behavioral or performance-based objectives, competencies, or
other explicit assessment devices.'

The Texas State Teacher Association countered with a bul-
letin to its members:

As directed by the House of Delegates,
TSTA is strongly opposing H.B. 1322 which
would take teacher education and certification control from TEA and the State Board
of Education and give it to the colleges.

In view of this conflict and political pressure, Texas Education
Commissioner, J.W. Edgar, has delayed implementation of CBTE
for 18 months.

Ethnic Minorities, Lay Groups, and Students

It is hardly news to point out the increasing militance
and organization of ethnic minorities in education. The current situation is very unlike the period when the current
certification and training requirements evolved. In one re-
spect, the performance concept moves counter to the demands of
minority groups to eliminate credentials and other formal requirements for teaching employment. On the other hand, minority
groups have argued that competence should be judged on one's
ability to perform or produce rather than college credits and
degrees. At any rate, PBTE could have a large impact on who
gets jobs - and teaching jobs for all ethnic groups are getting
scarce compared to the number of trainees. Bernard Bard puts
the New York experience in this perspective.

All of which is to say that there may be
moral posturing on both sides of the New
York struggles; that beneath the verbiage
is an economic interest. The defenders of

14

the present arrangement speak of the
schools as a potential 'porkbarrel'
and say the NAACP is simply out to
get its hands on a $90 million barrel.
This is, of course, hyperbole. The
man on every payroll says he got there
because of "merit;" it is always the
other guys who are trying to bring in
the spoils system.[16]

The probable minority position will be to establish different performance criteria for minority teachers and students.
They will also want blacks to have a major role in evaluating
the performance of other blacks. PBTE can expect an early
court challenge under the new regulations of the Federal Equal
Employment Opportunity Commission. The empirical validity
issue can not be sidestepped or hidden under political and
value compromises. The courts will need sufficient evidence
that performance standards are related to job performance and
success. As Popham points out we have yet to devise adequate
teacher competence assessment systems.[17] Obviously, ethnic
minorities have several power bases (especially at the federal
level) from which they can demand and receive concessions from
PBTE adherents. At the very least, they should be able to delay implementation.

Parental groups correctly contend that they lack influence
in the present system. Often their views clash with the organized professionals. Parents cite examples of ineffective
teachers who are protected by their colleagues from dismissal.
As we have seen, the criteria of competence is not merely a
technical or professional issue, it goes to the heart of conflicting values. California's Teacher Evaluation Law ("Stull
Bill") specifies teachers should be evaluated on how well they
maintain "proper control and a suitable learning environment."[18]
Some parental groups and state legislators envision teacher
organizations as just another employee special interest lobby
that is not congruent with the "public interest." Some lay
groups will want to use performance standards as a wedge to
change tenure policies - e.g. poor performance would result in
revocation of tenure.

Most state certification requirements were also established
long before the student involvement movement began. High school
students contend that they suffer the most from poor teaching
and can most directly report on the positive and negative consequences of performance. Students participate in many college
level decisions concerning hiring and promotion of faculty.

15

Teacher evaluation systems are now used in secondary schools as well. In short, once PBTE is proposed in general, students will come forward to assert their prerogative to determine the nature of required competencies and an evaluation of teacher performance. It will not be easy to ignore them or allow token participation. Both student and lay groups have used court suits to force more professional attention to their viewpoints. Indeed, some leaders in the PBTE movement want student involvement built into the evolution of PBTE programs.

State legislators and governors share to a significant extent some of the parental and student views. They are skeptical of the current standards, dissatisfied with tenure procedures, and unwilling to let "professional expertise" substitute for their judgment. Both California laws (Ryan and Stull) are a reflection of this legislative dissatisfaction. Both laws attempt to legislate specific standards and get into what has historically been considered the "professional domain." The California legislature took the initiative before the professional groups had an established position - much less a chance to form a coalition and unified position. This brings us back to the formal locus of control - state government. The outcome will vary state by state, but one professional group such as NCATE is likely to be the leading force in all states. The politics of education has changed drastically from even the early sixties when the initiative in most states rested with the professional groups.[19] This resurgence of state control since NCATE includes the state departments of education. In 1970 Stinnett summarized the new role of the state directors of teacher education in this manner:

> The new direction is away from inflexible adherence to the regulatory function and toward constructive, dynamic leadership - from the enforcement to a stimulation role.[20]

States are granting greater autonomy to preparation institutions and encouraging experiments including PBTE. Consequently, state departments are likely to exert more influence than they did at the height of the NCATE era.

Political Brokerage and PBTE

The preceeding sections have analyzed some of the numerous conflicting interests and actors who must participate in and have their views included in the detailed outcome of PBTE. The era is probably gone when a group like NCATE could or should

16

dominate the field. A likely scenario in many states is the
development of a standards board including all these viewpoints.
In some states the board will be advisory to the state board of
education; in others, like California, the board will make the
actual board policy decisions. If all these groups - teacher
organizations, government leaders, minorities, students, parents,
institutions of higher education, etc. - must participate and
be accommodated, we must acknowledge the necessity of adroit
brokerage and coalition formation. Someone must arrange the
compromises and concessions. This someone must be sure he or
she does not compromise away the essence of the performance concept or include in the implementation phase so many conflicting
objectives and details that the outcome is rendered meaningless.
Many federal demonstrations have failed in large part because
of this. Since PBTE will probably start in the demonstration
mode, our experience with federal demonstrations under EPDA is
instructive. As a recent report on EPDA evaluation stressed:

> In summary, then, it is difficult to mount
> effective evaluation efforts with a weak
> technology, an embryonic profession, and
> a weak institutional capacity. But import-
> ant as these problems are, they have not
> been the principal reason for BEPD's un-
> impressive evaluation record...the programs
> were developed in haste; they made impossibly
> broad claims; they were mounted without any-
> thing approaching the resources to manage
> complex and far-flung projects; little or no
> thought was given at the outset to what
> might be learned or how; programs were
> changed often; the changes are couched in
> sweeping rhetoric and bureaucratic reorgan-
> izations. As a result, little endures.[21]

In part what Cohen et al are describing is the outcome of a
political process where demonstrations are mounted quickly
because of political pressure and then loaded up with every
objective that some vocal interest group wants. Consequently,
a concept like teacher-centers is converted into a service
activity for minority children operating with parents, students,
and community organizations on a policy board. The essence of
teacher retraining is submerged in a potpourri of noble objectives championed by one group or another.

We can be sure in PBTE that conflict among interested
parties will emerge. A visible power struggle could cause

the public to become skeptical about the professed goals
of PBTE to improve the welfare of students. We can not pre-
dict whether the outcome will leave the essence viable. Appeals
to such traditions as separation of expert decisions from lay
decisions are not likely to impress militant ethnics or teachers,
state legislators, or parents. Everybody will want to be involved in almost everything. The stakes are high - jobs, pro-
motions, and educational effectiveness.

For example, what should be the proper ratio of participants in a PBTE policy board? On a 10 member board should
classroom teachers have 5 members or 3? There is no scientific
answer to such questions. Neither do theories of democracy or
political science help much. The outcome will vary in large
part state by state depending on such factors as the strength
of teachers' organizations and the legislature's satisfaction
with the past performance of the State Education Agency teacher
training effort. Those spearheading PBTE should be aware of
the different interests and viewpoints and plan for concessions
that must be made in order to build a coalition for the program.
In essence, a series of policy bargains will result that hope-
fully preserves intact the core of the concept. A crucial
issue is what group is going to take the initiative in brokerage for PBTE and what is the broker's prime policy goal? If
federal funds are relied upon to furnish demonstration momentum,
then the brokers may be federal officials operating with all
their policy constraints. On the other hand, state legislators
may seize on PBTE as a mechanism for revising tenure or reorient-
ing college courses.

In New York, the Regents must develop every four years a
master plan for postsecondary education. During their discussion of the most recent master plan, they concluded teacher
education was ineffective and, in the words of one regent, "a
disgrace." They seized upon PBTE as a "heuristic device" to
force broadscale reconsideration by the interest groups. The
regents' hearings on PBTE accomplished one objective of shocking
and alarming the teacher education groups. Their hearings
were dominated by opponents from teacher training institutions
and teacher organizations. These two groups coalesced on the
position that delay was needed until criteria could be developed.
Ethnic minorities split with some groups wanting specific criteria
and others pushing for ethnic living experiences as key.

In view of the underdeveloped stage of PBTE and the strong
opposition, the regents left the concept in their master plan
but delayed the deadline for implementation until September

18

1980. Whether the whole exercise will lead to a rethinking of teacher education in New York state remains to be seen. It did expose the contradictory pressures on teacher organizations. Teacher leaders recognize that many of their constituents have invested a great deal in college courses and would resist PBTE. On the other hand, they realize that PBTE offers a good chance for implementing judgments by the peers of teachers rather than university or government experts. In a recent position paper the New York State United Teachers stressed two flaws in the Regents' plan.

> The major flaw in this (planning) pro-
> cedure is that the local bargaining agent --
> the democratically elected representative of
> the teachers -- is not indicated as the repre-
> sentative of the teachers. Although the
> regulations do not preclude the bargaining
> agent from representing the teachers, we have
> evidence that some of the trial experiments
> in PBTE being conducted under the State
> Education Department have circumvented the
> local bargaining agent...
>
> The educational community must not fall
> victim to premature, partially developed
> programs that promise the public fantastic
> results on a shoe string budget.
>   (New York Teacher, June 10, 1973)

Representation and Educational Policy

The above analysis indicates the need for representation of several groups in setting policy for PBTE. In some states this will be a policy board; in other states it will be advisory. But what is representative, and how do we decide this individual is or is not "representative?" Often the term "representation" is bandied about with little attempt to define it consistently in a concrete situation. This final section will consider several alternative definitions in order to help PBTE intel-ligently choose among them.[22] Once a government or interest group chooses a preferred form of representation, then the theories below suggest how the governance board might be set up. Many states will probably opt for a mixture of these pure models.

The theoretical literature on representation is noteworthy for the persistence of puzzling conflicts and controversies.

There is no agreement among political scientists and theorists as to what representation is or means. Indeed various theorists present us with rival, mutually incompatible definitions.

One definition (Hobbes) sees a representative as someone who acts for another, who has been given authority to act by that other, so that whatever the representative does is considered the act of the represented?[23] Under this definition the representative need not consult the people's wishes, protect their interests or be responsible to them. In effect many representatives chosen for state level policy boards fit under this category. A professor of teacher education is chosen as "representative" of his field, but he acts as an individual and is not accountable to any group or constituency. The members of the California Commission for Teacher Preparation and Licensing (Ryan Act) fit this definition. The classroom teachers chosen are not accountable to a specific organization or constituency, neither are they famous charismatic leaders.

Another view of representation is, in Pitkin's words:

> ...someone who will be held responsible to
> those for whom he acts, who must account to
> them for his actions. What defines represen-
> tation is not an act of authorization that
> initiates it, but an act of holding-to-account
> that terminates it. Whereas Hobbes' represen-
> tative is a man free to do as he chooses,
> these writers see a representative as having
> new, special duties or responsibilities...
> *Neither view can tell us what is supposed to
> go on during representation.*[24]

Representatives of teacher organizations and ethnic minorities, for example, could be chosen for PBTE governance because of the likelihood that they will report back and be responsive to their organization. A policy board or advisory committee would then be chosen (probably elected) because it is an accurate part-by-part correspondence to the larger population for which it stands and is held accountable by this larger population. The proportion of classroom teachers or any group would be chosen to produce an accurate map or mirror of the entire educational community. The court suits resulting in one man, one vote and reapportioned state legislators follow this principle.

Often, however, education advisory groups represent contending groups symbolically. A symbol, though it represents by standing for something, does not resemble what it stands for. Consequently, a symbol is not a source of information about what it represents. Often token students or parents on a policy board provide symbolic representation of a large diverse group that we have no idea how to represent under any of the above concepts. Who really could represent parents of California school children? If we use the PTA head, it is really symbolic, given the way the PTA would handle the accountability question. In many ways, representativeness in education becomes a frame of mind. Symbolic representation is accepted because of the charisma or affective reactions of people to a particular person chosen for the position. The issue then becomes something similar to: "What makes people believe in a symbol, accept a certain person as leader and embodiment of the nation?"[25] Many "blue ribbon" advisory councils conform to this representational approach by appointing prestigious people who are not accountable to a constituency or based on one man, one vote.

A different way of looking at the problem is to explore the "proper conduct" of a representative - e.g. the activity of representing. The theoretical discussions polarize around what Pitkin calls the mandate-independence controversy: "Should (must) a representative do what his constituents want, or what he thinks best?" In effect, representation presents us with a paradoxical requirement that a thing (to be represented) be simultaneously present and not present. Given the state of theoretical development, one's position depends on the particular substantive issues involved. The more the political issues involve irrational commitment or personal preference rather than deliberation, the more the representative will need to consult the constituency preference. The more an issue is amenable to correct, objectively determinable solutions through rational inquiry, the more independence is needed; there is no use counting noses when the technical issues will yield to expertise.

But PBTE has elements of both of these - some of it can be determined objectively; other parts will necessitate value judgments. Perhaps the concept of PBTE can be separated into two overall components - one that is technical and measurable, another that is inherently value-laden. The representation scheme would then be different for the two components. The first could be settled through symbolic representation with a large number of technical experts who operate largely independent of any constituency groups. An ample full-time staff would be provided. The second component would also be enhanced by regional policy boards within large states like New York or California.[26]

Brokerage and Representation in Washington and Texas

The issues of brokerage and representation have both proven to be difficult and contentious in two states with CBTE implementation mandates. Both states have set up tripartite councils to plan and develop CBTE programs. The three members are the particular college campus, the school system and professional organizations. But both states have left vague the details of who is to be the broker and how are groups to be represented. The findings from a recent Washington study of experiences of Washington colleges and universities in implementing the 1971 guidelines indicate the following strengths and weaknesses related to this problem.

Strengths

- the concept provides an open system approach which allows for inputs from diverse groups at various stages of development.

- the concept, based on the parity principle, insures an equal voice among agencies.

Weaknesses

- the concept does not clarify the number of persons who should represent each agency.

- the concept does not clearly define the responsibilities of each of the participating agencies. There is no management system included for the assignment of accountability to any one of the participants.

- there seems to be serious confusion relative to the roles and responsibilities in the "umbrella consortium" approach.[27]

Washington relied on a model that implied that consensus could be reached among the three parties.

22

If the conflict is very deep, however, there is no explicit way
for one of the parties to overrule another or for arbitration.
This has led to protracted negotiations, long delays, and a
demand from participant observers to establish some kind of
"management system." Such a policy formulation system favors the
groups who have the most stake in the outcome and will spend the
most time and manpower in protracted discussions. As one
superintendent observed:

> My greatest concern with the 1971 Standards
> is that the viable concept of competency-
> based training programs has been delayed and
> even threatened by our insistence that we
> use an unworkable structure, i.e., the current
> consortium planning format.
>
> The first step in providing a workable system
> is to provide a structure which includes clearly
> defined lines of authority and responsibility
> along with appropriate channels.[28]

Texas has initially defined the campus as the senior part-
ner with the power to decide on the number and basis for representation of the schools and profession. But the teacher group
has already indicated that they will contest this.

Summary

This paper has raised a lot of issues but answered few of
them. Given the embryonic state of PBTE, this is to be expected.
We do not know if the concept can be implemented. Consequently,
we do not know the substance of the concept to be governed.[29]
Perhaps this can be worked out by the groups analyzed above.

The writer has stressed the following points which will
help resolve some of the crucial governance issues:

1) The evolution of influence in teacher preparation,
    certification, and promotion has favored the universi-
    ties and to a lesser extent state government (particu-
    larly state departments).

2) Since the current system was institutionalized, several
    interest groups have gained in strength and will demand
    a larger share of influence - e.g. teacher organizations,
    parent groups, ethnic minorities, students, state
    legislators, and state board members. Consequently,

some redistribution of existing influence is likely when PBTE is implemented.

3) These groups have different value perspectives between each other and within their own membership. PBTE is unlikely to have a research base that will resolve many value issues through empirical data. Consequently, value issues will become intensely political, engendering negotiations, bargaining, coalitions, and compromises.

4) The outcome of this political activity will vary according to the prior political culture in a state, the structure of statewide interest groups, and other state factors. A new national NCATE-type mechanism is unlikely because professional educators will be split according to such indices as humanists vs. behaviorists, classroom teachers vs. professors, and ethnic minorities vs. state department of education professionals.

5) Political theory provides no precise prescriptive or normative solutions for the optimal governance structures or procedures. Partial theories such as representation do suggest some appropriate directions.

6) Given the pluralistic and contending interest groups and the lack of research on proven "competencies," PBTE could become a negotiating slogan rather than an integrated conceptual framework. The motives and skill of political brokers will be of prime importance in determining the outcome.

7) Major policy trends such as tenure revision, affirmative action for minority employment, and the declining number of new elementary/secondary pupils will "spill over" into the bargaining on PBTE.

References

[1] Kirst, Michael and Decker Walker. "An Analysis of Curriculum Policy Making," *Review of Educational Research,* 41, no. 5 (Dec. 1971): 479-509. Kirst, Michael, and Frederick Wirt. *The Political Web of American Schools.* Boston: Little Brown, 1972.

[2] Cottrell, Donald P. *Selected Bibliography on Accreditation of Teacher Education,* ERIC Clearinghouse on Teacher Education, AACTE, 1970. See also T. M. Stinnett, ed., *Unfinished Business of the Teaching Profession in the 1970's,* Phi Delta Kappan, 1971; W. Earl Armstrong et al., *The College and Teacher Education* (Washington: American Council on Education, 1944).

[3] Stinnett, T. M. *A Manual on Certification Requirements for School Personnel* (Washington: NEA, 1967 Edition), pp. 1-4.

[4] Mayor, John R. *Accreditation in Teacher Education: Its Influence on Higher Education* (Washington: National Commission on Accrediting, 1965).

[5] Conant, James Bryant. "The Certification of Teachers: The Restricted State Approved Approach" (lecture), Charles W. Hunt lecture of AACTE, 1964.

[6] Stinnett, T. M. *Professional Problems of Teachers* (New York: MacMillan, 1968), p. 456. Margaret Lindsey, ed., *New Horizons for the Teaching Profession* (Washington: NEA-TEPS, 1961).

[7] Koerner, James. *Who Controls American Education* (Boston: Beacon, 1965), pp. 57-58.

[8] Combs, Arthur W. *Educational Accountability* (Washington: ASCD, 1972).

[9] Howsam, Robert. "The Governance of Teacher Education" (Washington: ERIC Clearinghouse on Teacher Education, 1972), p. 12.

[10] Barro, Stephen M. "A Review of the Power of Competency-Based Teacher Education." Paper prepared for Committee on National Program Priorities in Teacher Education, City University of New York, May 1972.

[11]Howsam, *op. cit.*, p. 16.

[12]Howsam, *op. cit.*, p. 18

[13]The National Commission on Teacher Education and Professional Standards, NEA. "Self-Governance For The Teaching Profession: Why?" Unpublished paper available in PBTE Clearinghouse, AACTE.

[14]The Writer is indebted to Professor Lorrin Kennamer, Dean of the School of Education, University of Texas for background on the Texas PBTE situation.

[15]Giles, Frederic T. "A Study of the Experiences of Washington Colleges and Universities in Implementing the 1971 Guidelines for Teacher Certification," unpublished.

[16]Bard, Bernard. "The Battle for School Jobs: New York's Newest Agony," *Phi Delta Kappan,* May 1972, p. 554.

[17]Popham, W. James. "California's Precedent-Setting Teacher Evaluation Law," in *Educational Researcher*, July 1972, pp. 13-15.

[18]*Ibid.*, p. 13.

[19]Berke, Joel S. and Michael W. Kirst. *Federal Aid to Education* (Lexington: D. C. Heath, 1972). Also Michael W. Kirst, ed., *Politics of Education at Federal, State, and Local Levels,* pp. 215-220.

[20]Stinnett, T. M. *A Manual on Certification Requirements for School Personnel in the United States* (Washington: NEA, 1970 Edition), p. 1.

[21]Cohen, David et al. *The Role of Evaluation in the Bureau of Education Prefessions Development* (Cambridge: Harvard Center for Educational Policy Research, 1971), pp. 340-341.

[22]Ideas for this section are drawn from Hanna Pitkin, ed., *Representation* (New York: Atherton, 1969).

[23]Hobbes, Thomas. *Leviathan.* Michael Oakeshott, ed. Oxford, England: Oxford Press, 1960.

[24]Pitkin, *op. cit.*, p. 9, underlined by author of this paper.

[25]Pitkin, *op. cit.*, p. 12.

[26]For a proposal on regional governance of PBTE see Mario Fantini, "The Reform of Teacher Education," *Phi Delta Kappan*, April 1972, pp. 474-478.

[27]Giles, *op. cit.*, p. 5.

[28]Beggs, Harold O., Superintendent Grand Coulee Dam Schools, January 15, 1973.

[29]The AACTE Board of Directors underlined this viewpoint in its June 1973 Policy Statement stressing the potential of PBTE and urging "a flexible and open position" for states until some basic concerns are resolved. See "Implementing Performance-Based Teacher Education At The State Level."

ABOUT AACTE

The American Association of Colleges for Teacher Education is an organization of more than 860 colleges and universities joined together in a common interest: more effective ways of preparing educational personnel for our changing society. It is national in scope, institutional in structure, and voluntary. It has served teacher education for 55 years in professional tasks which no single institution, agency, organization, or enterprise can accomplish alone.

AACTE's members are located in every state of the nation and in Puerto Rico, Guam, and the Virgin Islands. Collectively, they prepare more than 90 percent of the teaching force that enters American schools each year.

The Association maintains its headquarters in the National Center for Higher Education, in Washington, D. C. -- the nation's capital, which also in recent years has become an educational capital. This location enables AACTE to work closely with many professional organizations and government agencies concerned with teachers and their preparation.

In AACTE headquarters, a stable professional staff is in continuous interaction with other educators and with officials who influence education, both in immediate actions and future thrusts. Educators have come to rely upon the AACTE headquarters office for information, ideas, and other assistance and, in turn, to share their aspirations and needs. Such interaction alerts the staff and officers to current and emerging needs of society and of education and makes AACTE the center for teacher education. The professional staff is regularly out in the field--nationally and internationally--serving educators and keeping abreast of the "real world." The headquarters office staff implements the Association's objectives and programs, keeping them vital and valid.

Through conferences, study committees, commissions, task forces, publications, and projects, AACTE conducts a program relevant to the current needs of those concerned with better preparation programs for educational personnel. Major programmatic thrusts are carried out by commissions on international education, multicultural education, and accreditation standards. Other activities include government relations and a consultative service in teacher education.

A number of activities are carried on collaboratively. These include major fiscal support for and selection of higher education representatives on the National Council for Accreditation of Teacher Education--an activity sanctioned by the National Commission on Accrediting and a joint enterprise of higher education institutions represented by AACTE, organizations of school board members, classroom teachers, state certification officers, and chief state school officers.

The Association headquarters provides secretariat services for two organizations which help make teacher education more interdisciplinary and comprehensive: the Associated Organizations of Teacher Education and the International Council on Education for Teaching. A major interest in teacher education provides a common bond between AACTE and fraternal organizations.

AACTE is deeply concerned with and involved in the major education issues of the day. Combining the considerable resources inherent in the consortium--constituted through a national voluntary association--with strengths of others creates a synergism of exceptional productivity and potentiality. Serving as the nerve center and spokesman for major efforts to improve education personnel, the Association brings to its task credibility, built-in cooperation and communications, contributions in cash and kind, and diverse staff and membership capabilities.

AACTE provides a capability for energetically, imaginatively, and effectively moving the nation forward through better prepared educational personnel. From its administration of the pioneering educational television program, " Continental Classroom," to its involvement of 20,000 practitioners, researchers, and decision makers in developing the current Recommended Standards for Teacher Education, to many other activities, AACTE has demonstrated its organizational and consortium qualification and experiences in conceptualizing, studying and experimenting, communicating, and implementing diverse thrusts for carrying out socially and educationally significant activities. With the past as prologue, AACTE is proud of its history and confident of its future among the "movers and doers" seeking continuous renewal of national aspirations and accomplishments through education.

ABOUT THE TEXAS TEACHER CENTER PROJECT

The AACTE Committee on Performance-Based Teacher Education serves as the national component of the Texas Teacher Center Project. This Project was initiated in July, 1970, through a grant to the Texas Education Agency from the Bureau of Educational Personnel Development, USOE. The Project was initially funded under the Trainers of Teacher Trainers (TTT) Program and the national component was subcontracted by the Texas Education Agency to AACTE.

One of the original thrusts of the Texas Teacher Center Project was to conceptualize and field test performance-based teacher education programs in pilot situations and contribute to a statewide effort to move teacher certification to a performance base. By the inclusion of the national component in the Project, the Texas Project made it possible for all efforts in the nation related to performance-based teacher education to gain national visibility. More important, it gave to the nation a central forum where continuous study and further clarification of the performance-based movement might take place.

While the Texas Teacher Center Project is of particular interest to AACTE's Performance-Based Teacher Education Committee, the services of the Committee are available, within its resources, to all states, colleges and universities, and groups concerned with the improvement of preparation programs for school personnel.

AACTE BOARD OF DIRECTORS

Executive Committee:

William A. Hunter, President and Chairman of the Board; Dean, School
    of Education, Tuskegee Institute, Tuskegee Institute, Alabama 36088

George W. Denemark, Past President; Dean, College of Education, University of
    Kentucky, Lexington, Kentucky 40506

Sam P. Wiggins, President-Elect; Dean, College of Education, The Cleveland
    State University, Cleveland, Ohio 44114

Robert B. Howsam, Dean, College of Education, University of Houston,
    Houston, Texas 77004

Sister Fidelma Spiering, Academic Dean, Marylhurst College, Marylhurst,
    Oregon 97036

H. Kenneth Barker, Dean, College of Education, The University of Akron,
    Akron, Ohio 44304

Dean C. Corrigan, Dean, College of Education, The University of Vermont,
    Burlington, Vermont 05401

Pearlie C. Dove, Chairman, Department of Education and Psychology, Clark
    College, Atlanta, Georgia 30314

Samuel G. Gates, Executive Director, Trustees of the State Colleges in
    Colorado, 221 State Services Building, Denver, Colorado 80203

Henry J. Hermanowicz, Dean, College of Education, Illinois State University,
    Normal, Illinois 61761

Donald Hight, Professor of Mathematics, Kansas State College of Pittsburg,
    Pittsburg, Kansas 66762

Richard E. Lawrence, Dean, College of Education, The University of New
    Mexico, Albuquerque, New Mexico 87120

Arthur G. Martin, Superintendent of Schools, Moorestown Township Public
    Schools, 109 West Second Street, Moorestown, New Jersey 08057

Bert L. Sharp, Dean, College of Education, University of Florida,
    Gainesville, Florida 32601

Benedict J. Surwill, Dean, School of Education, Eastern Montana College,
    Billings, Montana 59101

Kenneth R. Williams, President, Winston-Salem State University, Winston-
    Salem, North Carolina 27102

Bob G. Woods, Dean, College of Education, University of Missouri-Columbia,
    Columbia, Missouri 65201

Liaison Members:

D. D. Darland, Associate Director, Division of Instruction and Professional
    Development, NEA, 1201 16th Street, N. W., Washington, D. C. 20036

Rolf W. Larson, Director, National Council for Accreditation of Teacher
    Education, 1750 Pennsylvania Avenue, N. W., Washington, D. C. 20006

AACTE PERFORMANCE-BASED TEACHER EDUCATION
PROJECT COMMITTEE

Chairman: J. W. MAUCKER, Vice President for Academic Affairs, Academic Affairs
           Office, Kansas State Teachers College, Emporia, Kansas 66801.

Vice-Chairman: DONALD J. MCCARTY, Dean, College of Education, University of
                Wisconsin, Madison, Wisconsin 53706.

WILLIAM W. BARR, Student, School of Education, University of Denver, Denver,
    Colorado 80210.

ELBERT BROOKS, Superintendent of Schools, Metropolitan Schools, 2601 Bransford
    Avenue, Nashville, Tennessee 37203.

PATRICK L. DALY. Social Studies Teacher, Edsel Ford High School, 20601 Rotunda
    Drive, Dearborn, Michigan 48124.

K. FRED DANIEL, Associate for Planning and Coordination, State Department of
    Education, Tallahassee, Florida 32304.

WILLIAM H. DRUMMOND, Professor of Education, Department of Curriculum and
    Instruction, College of Education, University of Florida, Gainesville,
    Florida 32601.

TOMMY FULTON, Art Teacher, Jarman Jr. High School, Midwest City, Oklahoma 73110.

WILLIAM A. JENKINS, Dean, School of Education, Portland State University,
    Portland, Oregon 97207.

LORRIN KENNAMER, Dean, College of Education, University of Texas at Austin,
    Austin, Texas 78712.

DAVID KRATHWOHL, Dean, College of Education, Syracuse University, Syracuse,
    New York 13210.

MARGARET LINDSEY, Professor of Education, Teachers College, Columbia University,
    New York, New York 10027.

DONALD M. MEDLEY, Professor of Education, School of Education, University of
    Virginia, Charlottesville, Virginia 22903.

YOURA QUALLS, Head, Humanities Division, Tuskegee Institute, Tuskegee Institute,
    Alabama 36088.

ATILANO VALENCIA, Head, Department of Education, New Mexico Highlands University,
    Las Vegas, New Mexico 87001.

PAUL VARG, Professor of History, Michigan State University, East Lansing, Michigan
    48823.

Liaison Representatives:

THEODORE ANDREWS, Associate in Teacher Education, Division of Teacher Education and
    Certification, New York State Department of Education, Albany, New York 12204
    (Multi-State Consortium).

NORMAN DODL, Associate Professor, Department of Elementary Education, Florida State
    University, Tallahassee, Florida 32306 (Elementary Education Model Program
    Directors).

HARLAN FORD, Assistant Commissioner of Education, (or TOM RYAN) Texas Education
    Agency, Austin, Texas 78701.

NORMAN JOHNSON, Chairman, Department of Education, North Carolina Central University,
    Durham, North Carolina 27707 (Southern Consortium).

KYLE KILLOUGH, Director, Texas Education Renewal Center, 6504 Tracor Lane, Austin,
    Texas 78721 (Texas Teacher Center Project).

DONALD ORLOSKY, Professor of Education and Associate Director of Leadership Training
    Institute, University of South Florida, Tampa, Florida 33620.

BENJAMIN ROSNER, Dean, College of Education, Temple University, Philadelphia,
    Pennsylvania 19122.

ALLEN SCHMIEDER, Chief, Operations Coordination, National Center for Improvement
    of Educational Systems, U. S. Office of Education, Washington, D. C. 20202
    (Office of Education).

EMMITT SMITH, Vice President, Program Development and Resources, West Texas State
    University, Canyon, Texas 79015 (Texas Teacher Center Project).

PUBLICATION ORDER FORM FOR PBTE PAPERS

Number of Copies	PBTE Series	
_____	#1	"Performance-Based Teacher Education: What Is the State of the Art?" by Stan Elam @ $2.00
_____	#2	"The Individualized, Competency-Based System of Teacher Education at Weber State College" by Caseel Burke @ $2.00
_____	#3	"Manchester Interview: Competency-Based Teacher Education/Certification" by Theodore Andrews @ $2.00
_____	#4	"A Critique of PBTE" by Harry S. Broudy @ $2.00
_____	#5	"Competency-Based Teacher Education: A Scenario" by James Cooper and Wilford Weber @ $2.00
_____	#6	"Changing Teacher Education in a Large Urban University" by Frederic T. Giles and Clifford Foster @ $3.00
_____	#7	"Performance-Based Teacher Education: An Annotated Bibliography" by AACTE and ERIC Clearinghouse on Teacher Education @ $3.00
_____	#8	"Performance-Based Teacher Education Programs: A Comparative Description" by Iris Elfenbein @ $3.00
_____	#9	"Competency-Based Education: The State of the Scene" by Allen A. Schmieder (jointly with ERIC Clearinghouse on Teacher Education) @ $3.00
_____	#10	"A Humanistic Approach to Performance-Based Teacher Education" by Paul Nash @ $2.00
_____	#11	"Performance-Based Teacher Education and the Subject Matter Fields" by Michael F. Shugrue @ $2.00
_____	#12	"Performance-Based Teacher Education: Some Measurement and Decision-Making Considerations" by Jack C. Merwin @ $2.00
_____	#13	"Issues in Governance for Performance-Based Teacher Education" by Michael W. Kirst @ $2.00

BILLED ORDERS: Billed orders will be accepted only when made on official purchase orders of institutions, agencies, or organizations. Shipping and handling charges will be added to billed orders. Payment must accompany all other orders. There are no minimum orders.

DISCOUNTS: A 10 percent discount is allowed on purchase of five or more publications of any one title. A 10 percent discount is allowed on all orders by wholesale agencies.

Payment enclosed_____   Amount_____

                                        Purchase Order No._____

NAME_____
                        (Please print or type)

ADDRESS_____ZIP CODE_____

Please address: Order Department, American Association of Colleges for Teacher Education, Suite #610, One Dupont Circle, Washington, D. C. 20036.

ORDER FORM FOR RECENT AACTE PUBLICATIONS

Number of
Copies

"The Profession, Politics, and Society" (1972 Yearbook)

_____   Volume I and Volume II @ $6.00

_____   Volume I (Proceedings Only) @ $4.00

_____   Volume II (Directory Only) @ $3.00

_____ "Power and Decision Making in Teacher Education" (1971
         Yearbook) @ $6.00

_____ "What Kind of Environment Will Our Children Have?" @
         $2.50

_____ "Social Change and Teacher Education" @ $2.50

_____ "Systems and Modeling: Self-Renewal Approaches to Teacher
         Education" @ $3.25

_____ "Excellence in Teacher Education" (Limited Supply) @ $1.00

_____ "Beyond the Upheaval" @ $1.00

_____ "In West Virginia, It Is Working" @ $2.00

_____ "Educational Personnel for the Urban Schools: What Differen-
         tiated Staffing Can Do" @ $2.00

_____ "An Illustrated Model for the Evaluation of Teacher Education
         Graduates" @ $2.00

BILLED ORDERS: Billed orders will be accepted only when made on official
purchase orders of institutions, agencies, or organizations. Shipping and
handling charges will be added to billed orders. Payment must accompany all
other orders. There are no minimum orders.

Payment enclosed_____   Amount_____

                                  Purchase Order No._____

NAME_____
                   (Please print or type)

ADDRESS_____

_____ZIP CODE_____

Please address: Order Department, American Association of Colleges for Teacher
                 Education, Suite #610, One Dupont Circle, Washington, D. C.
                 20036.